RELIGIONS OF THE WORLD

I Am Shinto

❋ NORIKO S. NOMURA ❋

The Rosen Publishing Group's
PowerKids Press™
New York

Published in 1996 by The Rosen Publishing Group, Inc.
29 East 21st Street, New York, NY 10010

First Edition

Book design: Erin McKenna and Kim Sonsky

Photo credits: Cover © Bill Tucker/International Stock; p. 4 © Caroline Wood/International Stock; pp. 7, 12, 19 © Larry Dale Gordon/Image Bank; p. 8 © Jonathan Pite/Liaison International; p. 11 © Wolfgang Kaehler/Liaison International; p. 15, 16 © Wendy Chan/Gamma Liaison; p. 20 © Miwako Ikeda/International Stock.

Nomura, Noriko S.
    I am Shinto / Noriko S. Nomura.
        p.   cm. — (Religions of the world)
    Includes index.
    Summary: A young Japanese American girl living in Honolulu with her family describes the beliefs and ceremonies of Shintoism.
    ISBN 0-8239-2380-0
    1. Shinto—Juvenile literature. [1. Shinto.] I. Title. II. Series: Religions of the world (Rosen Publishing Group)
BL2220.N656 1996
299'.561—dc20
                                                96-6979
                                                CIP
                                                  AC

Manufactured in the United States of America

Contents

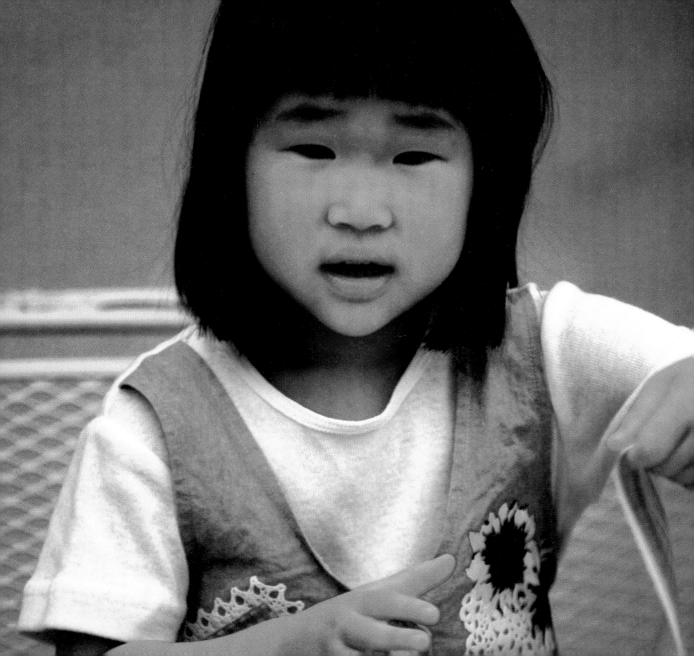

Being Shinto

My name is Yasuko. I live in Honolulu. My grandparents came from Japan. I am Shinto.

Shinto is the official religion of Japan. It is a very old religion. Shinto is based on traditions passed from one **generation** (jen-ur-AY-shun) to the next. In the Shinto religion, our **ancestors** (AN-ses-terz) are very important.

◀ *Many Japanese Americans are Shinto.*

Kami

The Kami are spirits that live in nature. Sometimes they are also the spirits of our ancestors. My mother told me that the Kami are in beautiful things like waterfalls and mountains. The word Shinto means "the Kami way." My mother and father have taught me that the Kami affect our lives in many ways.

The Kami are believed to live in beautiful things in nature. ▶

Purification

One of the most important acts we perform in Shinto is **purification** (pyur-if-ih-KAY-shun). Purification means cleansing. We make ourselves pure to show our respect to the Kami. Before we pray or enter a **shrine** (SHRYN), we wash our hands and mouths with water and sometimes salt. We use salt and water at other times too to cleanse ourselves and the spaces where we pray.

◀ *A person washes his hands and mouth before praying at a shrine such as this one.*

Shrines

Shrines are special buildings where the Kami come to meet with us. We go to the shrine to pray. All shrines have a special gate called a **torii** (toh-REE-ee). We ring a bell and sometimes we clap our hands to let the Kami know we are there. We thank the Kami who are there for all the good things they do for us. We ask them for help when we need it.

Shrines are special places where people can pray. ▶

Kami Dana

In our house we have a special place called a "Kami Dana." It is a wooden shelf. We keep a special piece of paper on the shelf. On the paper is the name of a Kami. This Kami may be an ancestor, or it may be another Kami. Sometimes we put a branch of evergreen there too. The evergreen stands for long life.

In the morning my mother and I place a bowl of rice and water on the Kami Dana for the Kami. These are offerings to show that we **honor** (ON-er) the Kami.

◀ *Children learn the traditions of Shinto from their parents and grandparents.*

13

The New Year

The new year is a great festival time in the Shinto religion. We celebrate it for three days. The most important part of the holiday is **Hatsumode** (HAT-soo-mo-day). This is our first visit to the shrine for the new year. We take rice cakes, **sake** (SOCK-ee), and tangerines to the Kami. When we reach the shrine, my parents let me ring the bell at the entrance.

Shinto families go to the shrine to celebrate the new year. ▶

Hina Matsuri

The Hina Matsuri, "the doll festival," is a fun celebration. It is especially fun for girls. My parents honor their daughters, me and my sister, Keiko. We set out dolls in our house. The dolls represent the **emperor** (EM-per-er) and his **court** (KORT). My family adds a new doll every year. My sister and I dress up in special clothes and we go to the shrine.

Boys have a "boy's day." My brother and father hang a windsock outside in the shape of a Koi fish or goldfish. The Koi fish stands for strength, courage, success, and long life.

◀ *Shinto girls wear traditional Japanese clothes when they dress up for the Hina Matsuri.*

Marriage

My brother Kenzo is getting married. It is an important day in his life and for his bride, Noriko. She will wear three beautiful **kimonos** (ki-MO-noze) on that day. The first one is pure white. The second one is bright red with a gold dragon on it. The third one is the kimono that she will wear to begin her new life with Kenzo. Noriko and Kenzo will each drink sake, and the family will say wedding vows for them.

Weddings are happy times for Shinto couples. ▶

7-5-3 Festival

When I was three, and this year, when I turn seven, my mom and dad will take me to the shrine. I will dress up in a bright red kimono. When we get to the shrine, we will thank the Kami that I am healthy. I will pray for blessings in the future. We buy a special candy at the shrine called **chitoseame** (chee-toh-say-AH-may). It means "1000 years of age" or "long life" candy. Boys, like my brother, do this when they are five.

◀ *Shinto children celebrate their health and future in special ceremonies when they are certain ages.*

Seijin-no-Hi

Seijin-no-Hi (say-jeen-NO-hee), a most special day, will come when I am 20 years old. It means "coming-of-age day." It is the day when I and many other people will become adults. It is a national holiday in Japan. On that day, everyone who is turning 20 years old that year dresses up in his or her best clothes. We visit a shrine and pay our respects to the Kami. We have a photographer take an official portrait on that day. From then on, we are adults in Shinto life.

Glossary

ancestors (AN-ses-terz) People in your family who lived before you.

chitoseame (chee-toh-say-AH-may) "1000 years of age" candy.

court (KORT) The emperor's staff of people.

emperor (EM-per-er) Ruler of country or empire.

generation (jen-ur-AY-shun) All the people born at a certain time.

Hatsumode (HAT-soo-mo-day) Celebration of the new year.

honor (ON-er) Respect.

kimono (ki-MO-no) Traditional Japanese robe.

purification (pyur-if-ih-KAY-shun) Cleansing.

sake (SOCK-ee) Rice wine.

Seijin-no-Hi (say-jeen-NO-hee) Coming-of-age day.

shrine (SHRYN) Place of worship.

torii (toh-REE-ee) Gate guarding a shrine.

Index